Wisdom

A Celebration of the
Intelligence and Beauty of Cats

K. J. VOEGELI

ISBN
979-8-89633-102-5 (Paperback)
979-8-89633-103-2 (eBook)

Page Solutions
541 Buttermilk Pike
Crescent Springs, KY 41017

I AM THE NIGHT WATCHMAN

I arise when everyone's lying
In state in their blanketed rooms.
I clamber down to the front window
And peer through the gathering gloom.
They say I'm a witch's familiar,
But familiar am I only with night;
I can conjure my own inner demons
Whenever my instincts take flight.
I scour the basement for critters,
I listen for noises at walls.
There is a small door across the front hallway floor That allows me out when nature calls.

At times I will venture in silence
Through the dark of a crisp autumn eve.
And the wind gently rustles my hair
While my feet crackle on the dry leaves.
I can spy all the shadows lurking
Round the edge of the stone garden wall;
Long ingers creep threateningly forward
As the moonbeams throw light on them all.
All at once I see movement before me,
So sudden and quick, I discern –
I lunge sure and swift, and the shadows do lift
From the ground never to return.

They say I am the night watchman,
A useful and valuable friend.
'Tis my role to protect my familiars,
And this I shall do til my end.

4

HIDDEN

I hear a voice calling me,
Coaxing me down the stairs.
This is where they put me down
For the night.

I tenaciously guard my post,
Shrinking back into the shadows,
Curling up into the furthest corner
Under the bed, sinking into the carpet.

I smile knowingly.
I'm not such a bad girl.
I remain bundled up, quiet as a dream,
So as not to attract suspicion.
They trust me very little;
I trust myself more.

IN MEMORIAM

Today I sit here on my own
Upon an autumn day.
The sky is grey as winter's chill
And a good friend's passed away.
I gaze upon her photo fair,
A lively and attractive puss,
With grey and black flecks in her hair;
She was never one to make a fuss.

Her company, as I recall,
Was lavish and devoted.
When I lay injured from a fall,
Or ill upon my bed,
She would drape her clawless mitten paws
Across my lap and hands,
While I stroked along her soft, warm jaw.
Her tongue felt like wet sand.

Her collar now sits on the shelf
Next to her tiny porcelain urn.
When I look there I forget myself
And to happier days my thoughts do turn.

It seems, Puss, that your presence here
Opened up my heart enough to mend
The loss of my special little dear
By offering me a new cat friend.

HALLOWEEN HOWL

The moon is full
And I feel the pull
Of a common feline call.
There's a place we meet
'Bout a hundred feet
From the ancient farmyard wall.

In the dead of night
It is such a sight
To see forty cats at once
Come from left and right
Through the cold twilight
To perch on the old wood fence.

In the gleam of our eyes
We see a form rise
From the depths of the hard dirt row.
It cackles and screams
Like the worst of your dreams
As it sails on a stick to and fro.
Ghostly shapes unfurl
From the fog and swirl,
Their horrid moans wailing in key.
And we dance on our toes in the chilly dry rows,
Howls rising in chorus with glee.

Men would recoil
At the sight of our toil,
The most horrible sight they would see.
They would cower in fright,
And run home in the night,
From our Halloween jamboree.

AT PLAY IN THE SUMMER

It's all so quiet, so wonderfully still,
And the breeze is scented with rose.
I am roaming outdoors in my backyard domain Near the bench where I usually doze.

A butterfly sits where I often lie,
Its dainty paper wings displayed.
A gentle gust sends it fluttering off,
Its brilliant bold colours on parade.

I chase like the kitten I used to be,
And the butterfly dances to and fro.
My paws fly out with lightning speed
But they close on air – nothing there below.

At once, from the corner of my eye
I glimpse a tail climbing up the tree.
I sprint, and my claws catch on the bark,
But the squirrel is quick and he evades me.

A red bird joins it in the branches,
Balancing on a slim knobby limb.
Its chirps send shivers to the end of my tail,
And I squeak and chatter in chorus with him.
Something buzzes me on my nose,
Its little red and black wings outspread.
I lose my grip as I swat at it,
Falling backward onto a grassy bed.

I decide right then to stay there a while,
Chewing the grass and admiring the hum
Of the toads, insects and human refrain
As my shadow grows long in the rising sun.

IN AND OUT

I look in at the ireplace
As the wood beneath me stings.
I'm yearning for some sweet repose
Among my bedding things.
I cried for hours at supper,
And in my eagerness to explore
I failed to notice the tiny flakes
A-falling past the door.
Curiosity satisied
I yowled for them in vain.
My outstretched paw searched frantically For a crack in the windowpane.
The cold bites hard at my delicate feet,
And the wind chews at my skin.
I now cry for my soft, warm bed –
Please, someone, won't you let me in?

CAT WITH ITS OWNER

The lights are low, and a softening glow
Swaths the harsh dark edges in gold.
My companion and I settle down to lie
In a soft chair free from the cold.

My legs stretched out, with your warm, wet snout
Nestled into my shoulder to rest.
My hand's clasped round your form, and the sound
Of your purrs resonate in my breast.

In your deep blue eyes, I now realize,
Bring the memory of a pet long passed.
I cannot recall, but I was very small;
It was then that the dye was cast.

I would lie in my bed, dreams illing my head,
And my pet would lay curled in my arm.
She'd guard my small cot,
Growl and hiss at the lot
Who'd dare to intend any harm.

As I stroke your soft face, and my long ingers trace
The brown silky sheen of your tail,
Your whiskers brush my chin, and you slyly grin
As sleep falls over us like a veil.

Ever since I was young I was always among
Those who cherished feline company.
This much is true, I will look after you,
As I'm sure you will look after me.

AT THE CLINIC

I peer cautiously out of my black-barred cage,
The floor is linoleum tile.
I must be examined because of my age;
I haven't been here in a while.

I knew from the moment that they brought it out
I was going to despise this trip.
They grappled me and held onto my legs
Before I could give them the slip.

The odour is sterile, the table is cold,
And my owner bear-hugs me in case.
They are gentle with me but I know what they do
Whenever you visit this place.

They banged on the bottom and dragged me clean out;
I've been prodded and needled straight through.
You can be doubly sure when we return home
I am no longer speaking to you.

CATS AND DOGS

Cats and dogs are our good friends,
Requiring a good part of our care.
And in return they always have
Unconditional love to share.

Dogs are loyal, playful
And with exuberance abound.
Cats are loyal to a fault,
Their judgment always sound.

A cat may scratch you angrily
But is typically quite calm.
It's quiet for the most part
And is usually close to home.

Cats require basic care,
The rest they do themselves.
They are small enough to cuddle
Or to sit amongst your shelves.

They are smart enough to reason with,
Though at times they listen not.
Cats often very quickly learn
To look out for their lot.
Cats are very loving,
But to earn their trust and cheer
One must treat them all with kindness,
Or they soon will disappear.

LIFE OF REILLY

I see you sprawled upon the sill,
Sunlight warming your silver hair.
And slumber as you always will
Whilst sunrays round about you flare.

Your life of ease befuddles me
As I sprint back and forth in haste.
You have no worries, all carefree;
For you mornings are to be embraced.

You do not care for bills and such;
Your shopping sprees are very few.
Phone calls do not faze you much,
As no one will be calling you.

I often envy your daily rest;
I'd gladly swap you for your share,
And I'd surely feel immensely blessed
To have a throw and a comfy chair.

So, my darling pet, I must
Return to work and wage the ight.
I will be long away, I trust;
You won't see me until tonight.

OUR OLD CAT

My mother once had an old tabby.
This gentle animal went by the name of Kitty,
A moniker placed on her by
My then-three-year-old sister.

She lived next door to us, a timid kitten
Residing with a rowdy young man
Who constantly hosted loud parties.

My mother felt sorry for her,
And would leave a dish of cat food behind our mailbox.
Eventually the dish was moved indoors,
Where my sister and I marvelled as
This small cat emptied the bowl.
Eventually she became part of the family,
Having four kittens herself, two of whom we kept.

Through the years she became queen
Of the household, outliving her kittens,
Dying from diabetes at the age of 17 years, 8 months.
My mother had her cremated and her little white urn
Sits in prominence on her dresser.

In memory of a loving, even-tempered friend
Who kept her company in sickness and in health.

AT THE TABLE

My plate is full at the supper hour
And I've settled into dine.
Now a delicate mew Has given me a clue
I shan't go unnoticed this time.

Oh kitty, the meat that's so tender and rare
That you smelled from your perch in my room
Has attracted your gaze
And your incessant plays
For a taste of this scrumptious perfume.

It seems that when I replenished your store
You felt it fell short of your due.
So now I must hear Constant whines in my ear
And your pushy paw taps on my shoe.

As always, I give a small portion of steak,
Handed lovingly to my fat cat.
Should this beast not enjoy
The same treats as this boy
Who shares all of his comforts at that?

ASLEEP

This is my pillow, my chair.
Can't you see I'm sleeping?
I have one eye open and
I'm watching you.

I will turn my back on you
If you attempt to disturb me;
I will not be budged.

Ignore my warning at your own risk –
You'll receive a sharp gaze and a nasty hiss,
Maybe even a bite.

Do not underestimate me, human.
I am your rival.

BOEHMER THE ORNERY CAT

I once had a little black bomber;
Boehmer was this grumpy cat's name.
Boehmer as in rhymes with streamer,
And these she would eat just the same.

She'd annoy our old reigning tabby,
Who'd snarl and spit at her shadow.
It was said that her playful advances
Helped put the poor old girl below.

She'd chew paper and boxes and tinsel,
Which we stopped using on our Christmas trees.
She'd knock over vases, and bite you and
Hit if you got in her space, if you please.

She never suffered fools gladly,
And would not hesitate to defend
Her right to a couch takeover –
God help those who'd not comprehend.

In Heaven now; God must have His hands full
Keeping up with our bossy old brat.
They said she died 'cause her heart was too big –
Well, we could have told them that.

THE PUSS WHO TALKED TOO MUCH

First thing in the morning when no one's awake
She comes to greet you in bed.
She jumps heavily onto the mattress and then
Sits and squawks at you next to your head.

She is bold, black and handsome,
A rare masculine beauty, I mean.
And her voice is a remnant of chorus hall brash,
Full of smoke from the cigarette scene.

To follow you round is her duty in life,
Her devotion complete and sincere.
She indelibly knows it was her that you chose,
And reminds you quite often now here.

Don't be angry or biting with her,
Although it is hard to resist.
When you sit down with her and pay her some mind
Is the only time she will desist.

CELEBRATING CATS

There never was a more inscrutable race
Of animals on this earth.
English poets revere their cats, but here
There is a frightful dearth
Of both prose and narrative that
Promotes the sharp and regal cat.

COMFORT

Your angora fur is like a
Favourite sweater worn for sheer delight.
Your mound of paws enclose my hand
Like the warmest gloves of wool.
Your eyes are flames of molten gold water
That I bathe in before sleep.
Your purr is like a musky cologne
That lulls the wearer into hypnotic comfort.

IN THE FIRELIGHT

Your shadow casts an eerie glow
Upon my hearth of stone.
Your company gives warmth to me,
It means I'm not alone.

COMPANIONSHIP

As the wind picks up outside
You and I wrap ourselves around
Each other like two blankets tied in knots.

We both insist on exquisite comforts,
Plush bedding, good foods,
So we spoil ourselves with many
Material things, not holding back.

I use you as my example to live life
As richly and as deeply as possible.

TO AN ACQUAINTANCE

As the center of attention
You command a hefty fee.
Your social acumen dictates
The law here, and that's "me".

Your annoyance is condemning,
You don't hesitate to sting.
But it's pitiful when you're
Corrected, you sorry little thing.

But we have an understanding,
You and I, and it's enough
To know the glue that holds us
Side by side is, inarguably, love.